# SOMETIMES I HAVE T
## VERSES FROM THE PSALMS O

BY ELSPETH CAMPBELL MURPHY
ILLUSTRATED BY JANE E. NELSON

Chariot Books

SOMETIMES I HAVE TO CRY

ISBN: 0-89191-494-3
LC: 81-67738                                    Second printing, September 1982.

# SOMETIMES I HAVE TO CRY
## VERSES FROM THE PSALMS ON TEARS

BY ELSPETH CAMPBELL MURPHY
ILLUSTRATED BY JANE E. NELSON

You know what, God?

Sometimes I get sad and grouchy—like when I'm tired of my toys, and there's no one to play with, and I have nothing to do.

That's when I whine and cry a little.

But that's not when I feel the worst. You know
what the worst feeling is, God? It's when I feel so
deep-down sad that I can't stop crying.

Look at my pillow, God. It's all wet from my tears. Yesterday my dog got run over by a car. And now my crying just won't stop.

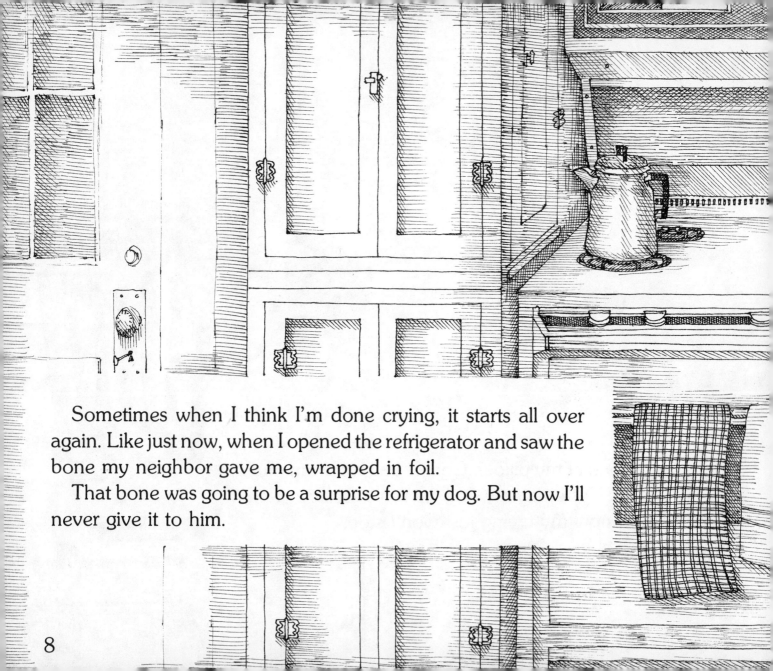

Sometimes when I think I'm done crying, it starts all over again. Like just now, when I opened the refrigerator and saw the bone my neighbor gave me, wrapped in foil.

That bone was going to be a surprise for my dog. But now I'll never give it to him.

You know, God, with all the people in the world, you must hear a lot of crying.

But you don't turn away and block up your ears. You're a good listener. And you understand.

My feelings are spread out in front of you the way we spread out papers at school. My sadness isn't hidden from you.

You know what, God? Sometimes when I'm sad, I close my eyes and pretend I'm a little baby again.

And then I imagine that you are a strong and gentle father, holding me close to you.

15

"There, there," I seem to hear you say. "Be still now, and just remember that I'm your God."

You let me know that it's all right to cry. And you help me know that I won't always be crying.

19

Remember the time I got really sick, and it seemed like I coughed all night long? That night was dark and scary—but then mom and I watched the sun come up, and everything seemed better.

Being sad is like a long, dark night, and being happy again is like the morning.

23

O God, you are my comforter, my
stick-beside-me friend.
How wonderful you are!